Visitation In Action

By R. O. SANBORN

Edited By:
Pastor D. A. Waite, Th.D., Ph.D.
Director, The Bible For Today, Incorporated

THE BIBLE FOR TODAY • COLLINGSWOOD, N.J.
900 Park Avenue
Collingswood, New Jersey 08108
BFT #4120

VISITATION IN ACTION
3rd Edition
R. O. Sanborn

ISBN: #978-1-56848-089-3
BFT #4120

THE BIBLE FOR TODAY PRESS++
900 PARK AVENUE
Collingswood, New Jersey 08108
U.S.A.

Edited by:
Pastor D. A. Waite, Th. D., Ph.D.
Bible For Today Baptist Church
Church Phone: 856-854-4747
BFT Phone: 856-854-4452
Orders: 1-800-John 10:9
Email: BFT@BibleForToday.org
Website:www.BibleForToday.org
Fax: 856-854-2464

We Use and Defend
The King James Bible

Publication and Formatting assisted by
The Old Paths Publications, Inc.
142 Gold Flume Way
Cleveland, GA 30528
Email: TOP@theoldpathspublications.com
Website: www.theoldpathspublications.com

DEDICATED TO:

ALL FAITHFUL WORKERS who are willing to use their TIME, TALENT, and ENERGY to reach people for the local church unto the LORD JESUS CHRIST.

"Therefore, my beloved brethren, be ye stedfast, unmoveable, always abounding in the work of the Lord, forasmuch as ye know that your labour is not in vain in the Lord." **(1 Corinthians 15:58)**

TABLE OF CONTENTS

FOREWORD

There are many books, pamphlets, and booklets on the subject of VISITATION. This book is unique.

It is not because there are not many others on this theme that THE BIBLE FOR TODAY publishes this particular booklet on VISITATION IN ACTION by R. O. Sanborn, but it is with a desire to provide for the average local church and Bible School a handy, succinct, suggestive, simple, useful, usable tool with which to inspire the people to ACTION.

Since this is a simple and easily-read booklet, with many suggestive ideas as to HOW TO DO IT, we sincerely hope that it will get a WIDE DISTRIBUTION in our fundamental churches and Bible Schools.

Why not give it a TRY?! Order one for EVERY TEACHER, EVERY YOUTH WORKER, EVERY DEACON, EVERY OFFICER, EVERY PROSPECTIVE VISITATION PERSON in your church!

Ask for quantity prices for this purpose and we will help you out.

In addition to this booklet's giving you a desire to go into Action on a visitation program, it gives you simple easy, direct METHODS and STEPS to get you STARTED. This is most important in this area of the Lord's work.

It is our prayer that many might be won to a saving knowledge of the Lord Jesus Christ by faith in Him as personal Savior through those who READ and then HEED the message of this booklet and go out and be good WITNESSES unto Jesus Christ!

Pastor D. A. Waite, Th.D., Ph.D.
Bible For Today Baptist Church
900 Park Avenue
Collingswood, N. J. 08108

ABOUT THE AUTHOR

Some words about R. O. Sanborn, the author of this booklet, are in order at this point.

FIRST, he has dealt with people of all kinds and descriptions for over 50 years in the business world, in various phases—in sales, sales promotion, sales management, recruiting, training, and building sales personnel. He knew from hard-working experience what it takes and how to start from "nothing" and build a successful sales organization.

SECOND, he has spent an equal number of years (50 or more) serving the Lord Jesus Christ in various ways, using his talents to inspire and interest people in serving Christ. He served in several Baptist churches as Bible School Superintendent and held almost every church office in the local church at some time or other. At the age of 25, he served as Chairman of the Board of Deacons. He was Chairman of the Board of Directors of BAPTIST BIBLE INSTITUTE of Cedarville, Ohio (the forerunner of what is now CEDARVILLE COLLEGE in Cedarville, Ohio). Following that, he also served as Trustee and Co-Chairman of the Board of Trustees of CEDARVILLE UNIVERSITY, Cedarville, Ohio (a school which was approved at the time by the General Association of Regular Baptist Churches-- G.A.R.B.C.), and was one of the pioneers in its beginning.

THIRD, he was saved at the age of 15 in a Baptist church in Cleveland, Ohio. He was a defender of the Faith as it is taught in the Bible, and knew what it meant to take a stand when it counted for the Lord. His motto, throughout his successful business career, and right up to the time of his early retirement in Florida, was: "ALWAYS, THE LORD FIRST and YOUR JOB SECOND!"

And beside all of the foregoing, it so happened that Mr. R. O. Sanborn, lived in St. Petersburg, Florida until his death in 1988. He was the editor's Father-in-law for over 40 years . I loved and appreciated Dad Sanborn's devoted stand for the Bible and for the Lord Jesus Christ throughout all of these years, but only during the last half of those years did I really seen WHY Dad was so strong in behalf of the various Biblical principles he stood for through the years. They are RIGHT principles, and what is more, they work in actual practice. And if upheld in the individual's life, they make them stand up for the Lord rather than compromise with the World, the Flesh, or the Devil.

Unless providentially hindered, I do not recall Dad Sanborn's ever missing a regular or special service of the local Baptist church of which he has been a member! When that church door opens, there he was, in his place, working, and worshipping the Lord. His local church was one of his FIRST loyalties, second only to the Lord Jesus Christ Himself. His example has inspired his Son-in-law to do likewise, and I'm sure has influenced many others as well to do the same.

I have seen him many times stand utterly ALONE on a point of principle where others would bend and bow to expediency. We certainly need more like R. O. Sanborn in our fundamental Baptist Churches AND OTHER INDEPENDENT Bible-believing churches around our country in times like these!

INTRODUCTION

This booklet is full of many ideas of "things" and "ways" to get a group of people into "HIGH GEAR" on a calling program. If properly supervised, it will become very profitable when placed into use in the local church.

Nothing takes the place of WORK. Things HAPPEN because someone made them happen! You, too, can be that someone.

Re-read Acts 2:42-47. Note some of these words:

"continued stedfastly"

"with one accord"

"favour with all people"

“praising God”

and many more words of encouragement in the things of Christ.

You will receive some very worthwhile ideas and suggestions from the pages of this booklet. Putting them into practice, you will find success for the Lord in the area of faithful, Christ-honoring visitation.

This booklet should be placed in the hands of the present VISITING COMMITTEE. If the church has no committee, Section XI tells how to START. The main thing is to BEGIN! The Pastor is ex-officio member at all meetings of the Visitation Committee.

VISITATION IS ACTION

Mark 16:15 *“And he said unto them, Go ye into all the world, and preach the gospel to every creature.”*

VISION ---TO SEE
Proverbs 29:18 *"Where there is no vision, the people perish: but he that keepeth the law, happy is he."*

FAITH --TO BELIEVE
Romans 10:13 *"For whosoever shall call upon the name of the Lord shall be saved."*

COURAGE --TO DO
Numbers 13:30 *"And Caleb stilled the people before Moses, and said, Let us go up at once, and possess it; for we are well able to overcome it."*

GO **DO** **GIVE**

"GO YE" – It's PERSONAL

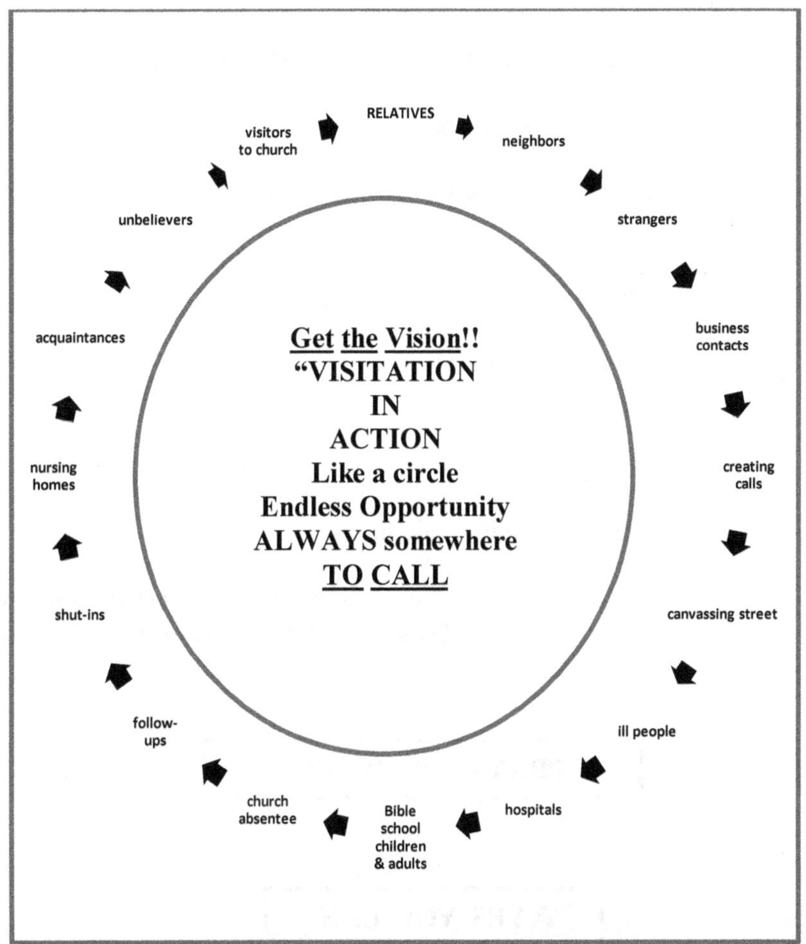

GOD USES INDIVIDUALS!

Luke 10:2 *"Therefore said he unto them, The harvest truly is great, but the labourers are few: pray ye therefore the Lord of the harvest, that he would send forth labourers into his harvest."*

"GO YE"

This booklet, "VISITATION IN ACTION," is a faith project.

Our desire, through the booklet is:

(1) to stir up the saints for service for our Lord so that they, in turn, would reach others.

(2) to reach many of the lost.

(3) to bring them to a saving knowledge of our Lord and Savior, Jesus Christ.

(4) to add thousands and thousands to our local churches.

What a REVIVAL this would be!

2 Corinthians 9:7 *"Every man according as he purposeth in his heart, so let him give; not grudgingly, or of necessity: for God loveth a cheerful giver."*

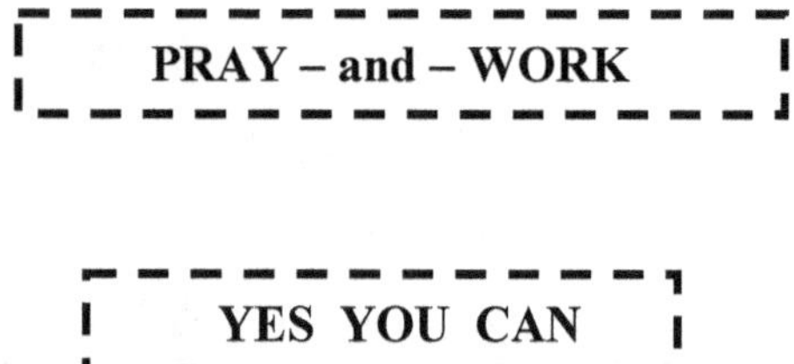
PRAY – and – WORK
YES YOU CAN

FORMULA FOR SUCCESS

"that thou mayest observe to do according to all that is written therein: for then thou shalt make thy way prosperous, and then thou shalt have good success." (Joshua 1:8c)

TRY THIS FORMULA

STEPS FOR S U C C E S S

(1) STUDY (The Plan) 2 Timothy 2:15

(2) GIVES KNOWLEDGE (About the Plan) Romans 8:28

(3) GAINS CONFIDENCE (In the Plan) Daniel 3:17, Philippians 4:13

(4) GENERATES ENTHUSIASM (Over the Plan Romans 12:1

IT GETS RESULTS!!!!

NOTHING TAKES THE PLACE OF WORK!

What we all need is to be MORE ENTHUSIASTIC in serving the Lord. The Apostle Paul said, in **2 Corinthians 13:5, to** "examine" and "prove." Put this in the light of our ENTHUSIASM in our service for Him, the Lord Jesus Christ.

The steps above show you how to become ENTHUSED in whatever the undertaking. Apply it to "VISITATION IN ACTION." You'll be surprised as to your RESULTS!

FIND YOUR PLACE—THEN GO TO WORK!

SECTION I

ACTION WORDS

"Knowing therefore the terror of the Lord, we persuade men; ..." **(2 Corinthians 5:11)**

In the Bible, the infallible, inerrant, verbally and plenarily inspired Word of God, we note many words of ACTION.

I want to bring three words to your attention as we apply them to this VISITATION IN ACTION plan.

GO DO, and GIVE are small words, but packed full of ACTION!

GO contains the first two letters of the Word, GOSPEL, and what a powerful effect the gospel has on people!

Romans 10:17 says, *"Faith cometh by hearing, and hearing by the Word of God."* Yes, the gospel, and faith in Christ as personal Savior changes lives. It changes your ways. It makes you a new person in Christ Jesus. Yes, it has an ACTION effect on your life.

When this takes place, another ACTION word comes into place, and that's found in James 1:22: *"But be ye DOERS of the Word, and not hearers only."*

Now we start to put into ACTION some of the things we have learned and will learn as we study the Bible.

The other word we mention is GIVE. We give of our time, our money, our talents, our willingnesss, to get a job done and a burning desire to see others learn about the Lord Jesus Christ through all our efforts, including passing out tracts and visiting people, inviting them to services.

Now, tackle this job of Church and Bible School visitation with a real GOAL in mind. DO everything in your power to get results and make it work. Just keep keeping after it weekly as you make your contacts, and you'll be surprised at the results.

N
O
W

I
S

T
H
E

T
I
M
E

THE GOAL IS TO SHOW "THE ROAD TO SALVATION" LEADING TO A SAVING KNOWLEDGE.

VISITATION IS THE CHURCH AND SUNDAY SCHOOL IN ACTION.

ACTION DOES NOT STAND STILL. IT GOES. It WALKS. It RUNS. It GETS THINGS DONE! FIND YOUR PLACE IN THIS PROFITABLE SERVICE.

BE A VOLUNTEER. DON'T WAIT TO BE DRAFTED. TO JOIN THIS GREAT ARMY OF GROUP LEADERS AND HELPERS, USE FORM #1. FILL IN AND HAND TO VISITATION CHAIRMAN.

YES YOU CAN!

SECTION II

WATCH THESE THINGS HAPPEN

R
E
N
E
W
E
D

I
N
T
E
R
E
S
T

Acts 2:47 *"Praising God, and having favour with all the people. And the Lord added to the church daily such as should be saved."*

1. RESULTS in your own growth.

2. RESULTS in Bible School attendance.

3. RESULTS in Church Services.

4. RESULTS in more loyalty and faithfulness to church, pastor, and all the saints.

5. RESULTS in workers who are DOERS, GOERS, AND GIVERS:

It takes WORK to get the MACHINERY running, and someone to give it a SHOT OF OIL occasionally. But it sure turns out the RESULTS! Why?—"Because you are giving the Lord your willingness to be used. Read Exodus 35:5, 21-22.

Let's make our local church and Bible School the best place this side of Heaven and let's DO everything possible to attract others as we "work together with the Lord."

"MACHINERY RUNNING" MEANS

1. The whole plan WORKING.

2. Visitation Chairman SUPERVISING.

3. Group Leader <u>CHECKING</u> their rolls.

4. Helpers <u>WORKING</u> at calling.

5. All contacts <u>BEING</u> <u>WORKED</u>.

6. All people <u>BEING</u> <u>CALLED</u> ON regularly.

"<u>SHOT</u> <u>OF</u> <u>OIL</u>" <u>MEANS</u>
Words of encouragement as you tackle the job.

SECTION III

PERSONAL HELPS

"For we are labourers together with God: ..." **(1 Corinthians 3:9)**

Y E S Y O U C A N

1. YOU MUST have the WANT TO.
2. YOU MUST WATCH YOUR ATTITUDE to be a successful worker.
3. YOU MUST know what you want and PLAN YOUR WORK.
4. YOU MUST PLAN how to GET RESULTS and PUT YOUR PLANS ON PAPER.
5. YOU MUST START AT ONCE to WORK YOUR PLAN.
6. YOU MUST be ENTHUSIASTIC about what you are doing, and have the right attitude to put it over.
7. YOU MUST remember that 90% of this job or any job is the ENTHUSIASM you give it.
8. YOU MUST GET EXCITED as you tackle your list of prospects.

Be one of the FIRST to VOLUNTEER!!

AIM HIGH! THINK BIG! HAVE MANY GOALS. As you reach one GOAL, SET UP ANOTHER!

SECTION IV

WHAT WE NEED

Romans 12:1 *"I beseech you therefore, brethren, by the mercies of God, that ye present your bodies a living sacrifice, holy, acceptable unto God, which is your reasonable service."*

O P P O R T U N I T I E S F O R A L L

1. WE NEED GROUP LEADERS.
2. WE NEED HELPERS.
3. WE NEED WILLING WORKERS.
4. WE NEED people who are FAITHFUL TO EVERY SERVICE of the Church.
5. WE NEED people who are LOYAL to the CHURCH, to the PASTOR, and to the PEOPLE. Most of all to the LORD! ("GO YE!").
6. WE NEED ACTIVE HOME MISSIONARIES.
7. WE NEED COUPLES and TEAMS.
8. WE NEED OLD and OLDER PEOPLE. There's a job for all.
9. WE NEED ALL WHO would do SPECIAL WORK FOR THE LORD.
10. WE NEED EVERY MEMBER being a COMMITTEE OF ONE TO CREATE at least ONE CALL PER WEEK.

"YES YOU CAN!"

"THINK YOU CAN, AND YOU WILL"

"HE THAT PROFITS MOST SERVES BEST"

"A CHURCH OF 1,000 MEMBERS NEEDS 100 GROUP LEADERS to HOLD THE LINE. TO MOVE FORWARD, INCREASE YOUR GROUP LEADERS AND HELPERS."

"IF YOUR CHURCH WANTS INCREASED ATTENDANCE, and IF YOUR CHURCH WANTS MORE WORKERS, then START AT ONCE WITH VISITATION IN ACTION"

SECTION V

WHAT TO DO

"But covet earnestly the best gifts: and yet shew I unto you a more excellent way." (***1 Corinthians 12:31)***

"For the perfecting of the saints,
For the work of the ministry,
For the edifying of the body of Christ:" ***(Ephesians 4:12)***

Be a CALEB or a JOSHUA, with FAITH TO BELIEVE and COURAGE TO DO!

The other TEN gave false reports. They were filled with NEGATIVE IDEAS. What pessimists! Their pessimism defeated their "GET UP AND GO."

They had NO VISION, NO TRUST, NO REWARD.

VISITATION IN ACTION is a positive, optimistic plan which will accomplish big things for churches that have a burning desire to reach people.

Here are some of the ways to reach people (see SECTION VI):

1. PASSING OF TRACTS –EVERYWHERE
2. INVITING PEOPLE TO ALL SERVICES—ANYONE
3. WITNESSING (Your Testimony)—EVERYBODY
4. LEADING PEOPLE TO A SAVING KNOWLEDGE OF THE LORD JESUS CHRIST—SPIRIT-LED
5. VISITING THE ILL AND THE SHUT-INS—WHOEVER

Everyone has a job to do. Find your place, then GO TO WORK!

TO BE SUCCESSFUL, ONE MUST HAVE GOALS. AS YOU REACH ONE GOAL, YOU SET UP ANOTHER.

A GOAL IS NOT A HITCHING POST!

IT'S SYSTEMATIC AND WORKABLE!

SECTION VI

VARIOUS WAYS TO CALL

T H I S

I S

A

D A I L Y

P L A N

"Let your SPEECH be alway with grace, seasoned with salt, that ye may know how ye ought to ANSWER every man." **(Colossians 4:6)**

1. CALLING by PERSONAL CONTACT.

That's FACE TO FACE with the prospect. It's the BEST METHOD of calling.Remember, GET IN, GET THRU, and then GET OUT

You're there for a reason. STATE IT. BE KIND. BE SINCERE. TACK IT DOWN. MAKE A FRIEND. BE A FRIEND.

2. CALLING BY PHONE.

Don't "visit" on the phone. This method is better than no contact at all. Make your phone call "SHORT AND SWEET." Don't forget what you phoned for. BE ENTHUSIASTIC. BE ALIVE. BE AWAKE. CREATE INTEREST.

3. CALLING BY LETTER.

Stick to your message. Most everyone can write a short note to someone. Be sure your CALL by letter "RINGS THE BELL."

KNOWLEDGE IS PUTTING YOUR LEARNING INTO PRACTICE

IT'S THE FOLLOW-THRU AND FOLLOW-UP THAT COUNTS.

FORGET YESTERDAY'S DEFEATS WORK TOWARDS TODAY'S VICTORIES!

"VISITATION IN ACTION" IS A TAILOR-MADE PLAN FOR EVERY BIBLE-BELIEVING CHURCH REGARDLESS OF SIZE.

Here's a few things "VISITATION IN ACTION" does:

1. FOR LARGER CHURCHES--It helps to HOLD THE LINE. It helps to develop more workers and teaches believers how to create calls.

2. FOR SMALLER CHURCHES--It helps them become larger because it's the VISITING of people by people that creates the INTEREST and GROWTH:

YES YOU CAN!

SECTION VII

VARIOUS KINDS OF CALLS

"[Y]e shall be WITNESSES UNTO ME both in Jerusalem, and in all Judaea, and in Samaria, and unto the UTTERMOST PART OF THE EARTH." **(Acts 1:8b,c)**

1. CALLS on ABSENTEES from services and from BIBLE SCHOOL, all departments.
2. CALLS on PARENTS of Bible School Children of all ages.
3. CALLS on those who are ILL.
4. CALLS on FRIENDS, both yours and those of others.
5. CALLS on NEIGHBORS.
6. CALLS on ACQUAINTANCES.
7. CALLS on RELATIVES.
8. CALLS on BUSINESS CONTACTS.
9. CALLS on UNBELIEVERS.
10. CALLS on BELIEVERS.

To sum it up: There is ALWAYS someone to CALL ON. Every house is a prospect. Learn how to create calls.

It is the VISITING of people that KEEPS the interest as well as GIVING the INTEREST.

"IT'S AN EVERLASTING JOB!"

LEARN HOW TO CALL—THROUGH CALLING!

The church and the BIBLE SCHOOL that learns how to see and meet people on a WEEKLY, DOOR-TO-DOOR CANVASS,

ALWAYS SOMEWHERE TO CALL

and that does it with a definite NUMBER to see EACH WEEK as a goal, that church or Bible School will show WEEKLY INCREASE (See SECTION XXI – XXII as to what to do .)

You set your goal for the entire church and Bible School first of all. Then you break it down for each individual to work towards their particular mark.

SEEING PEOPLE WEEKLY IS THE ANSWER
FOR STEADY GROWTH IN ATTENDANCE

SECTION VIII

THE PURPOSE FOR VISITING

E V E R Y   O N E   G R O W S

"The LORD hath done GREAT THINGS for us; whereof we are GLAD." ***(Psalms 126:3)***

1. VISIT to INCREASE ATTENDANCE at Church and Bible School.
2. VISIT as a GREATER OPPORTUNITY to BE A GOOD WITNESS to tell what God has done for you in Christ.
3. VISIT to LEARN HOW TO MEET PEOPLE (By passing out of tracts, for example). (Read SECTION #21)
4. VISIT to LEARN THE ART OF DEALING WITH PEOPLE.
5. VISIT to SHOW YOUR CONCERN for others and show them the way of SALVATION.
6. VISIT to "HOLD THE LINE" and MOVE FORWARD in your numbers and effectiveness.
7. VISIT to INCREASE your VISION of the lost.

FILL IN FORM #1. BE A VOLUNTEER. We need one group leader for every three families in the church or Bible School. On the average, there are about 10 people in three families. (See SECTION #24)

KNOW WHAT TO DO—and then LEARN THE ART OF DOING IT!

"Teaching them to OBSERVE all things..." (Matthew 28:20)

READ to LEARN what to do. Then DO IT!

1. CONTACTING PEOPLE (Read SECTION XXI)

2. CREATING A DESIRE (Read SECTION XXII).
3. WHAT TO DO WITH ABSENTEES (Read SECTION XXIII)

You'll develop the ART OF DOING by working at the things mentioned in these pages above.

SECTION IX

WHAT IS NEEDED

SUPERVISION IS NEEDED

"Let all things be done decently and in order." ***(1 Corinthians 14:40)***

1. The NEED of a VISITATION CHAIRMAN and a COMMITTEE which is Church-approved.
2. The NEED of a VISITATION COMMITTEE of only TWO with a CHAIRMAN which is large enough to begin with.
3. The NEED of GROUP LEADERS and HELPERS. These can be both men and ladies. They are selected by the VISITATION COMMITTEE.
4. The NEED of a BOOK OF FORMS to be furnished to each GROUP LEADER (#2 Forms) to keep records of services on his list. Use a new form each week. The purpose of these forms is to know who to call on when they are absent. (Order these from: THE BIBLE FOR TODAY or you can make your own copy on a copy machine.)
5. The NEED of HELPERS to work with their GROUP LEADER in contacting people who are absent, strangers, or canvassing streets to create a desire to visit the church or Bible School. These persons who express an interest, are then picked up by bus or car. GROUP LEADER SHOULD supervise their HELPERS and make sure everything is in order.

The Pastor is always an "EX OFFICIO" member.

T H E V I S I O N T O S E E

"Ask, and it shall be given you; seek, and ye shall find; knock, and it shall be opened unto you:" **(Matthew 7:7)**

YOU CAN GET WHAT YOU WANT "IF" YOU KNOW WHAT YOU WANT.

For example, "if" your Bible School wants to add 500 more in attendance, tell whether you want this growth in 30 days, 60 days, or 90 days. Plan WHEN.

Plan when you want these 500 people. First of all, you have to have 50 GROUP LEADERS to do the job. Each GROUP LEADER has to contact enough people through the methods suggested in "VISITATION IN ACTION" to get TEN EACH for sure.

To be able to get the TEN PEOPLE EACH it might take 100 CONTACTS and again it could take less.

Now, with every GROUP LEADER making his QUOTA of TEN, you have the 500, though it might take 5,000 CONTACTS to do the job.

Sure it takes planning and WORK.

PLAN—ANALYZE—and WORK!

PLAN HOW. ANALYZE WHAT IT TAKES. Then, GO TO WORK!!

Make up your mind to GET THINGS DONE! (see SECTION III—"Personal Helps"—and SECTION XVIII "Big Days")

SECTION X

THREE TYPES OF PEOPLE

"That ye be not slothful, but followers of them who through faith and patience inherit the promises." **(Hebrews 6:12)**

(This Plan is Like A)

T
A
S
T
Y

D
O
U
G
H
N
U
T

#1—THE PESSIMIST

Sees only the HOLE in the doughnut

Expects the WORST. Never tackles anything. Always finding FAULT. Everything WRONG. Filled with EXCUSES.

#2—THE OPTIMIST

SEES THE ENTIRE DOUGHNUT

Always sees the BRIGHT SIDE. HOPEFUL AND CHEERFUL and GRATEFUL for another day to tackle a NEW OPPORTUNITY. He KNOWS WHAT TO DO to get it done.

#3—THE "POSIMIST"

SEES THE ENITRE DOUGHNUT and EATS it

Has CONFIDENCE it can be done, and HE IS THE ONE who can DO IT. He is a "GO-GETTER." He FINDS A WAY or MAKES ONE. Never says "NO." He knows what to do and DOES IT!

LEARN TO BE A USABLE INDIVIDUAL

When selecting GROUP LEADERS and HELPERS, keep the above three types in mind.

The #1 TYPE will wear you out and tear every plan apart.Not much chance for that person until he or she learns to "WHOLLY FOLLOW THE LORD" (Joshua 14:8) and TRUST!

The DEACONS, TRUSTEES, TEACHERS, and OFFICERS will give you a good start on your "VISITATION IN ACTION" program. Set it up according to SECTION XI. The main thing is TO GET STARTED with what you have. It will gain momentum as you WORK at it. The more "POSIMISTS" you lineup to WORK, THE FASTER the plan will develop and GROW!

VISITATION is ACTION. ACTION by the CHAIRMAN—He is always RECRUITING, seeking out new workers, teaching and training these to do the job as outlined in this booklet.

It's a PERPETUAL PLAN. It's like rolling a hoop. You just don't stop! As the workers increase, so does the attendance.

SECTION XI

HOW TO START

A GOOD BEGINNING

"[T]hat thou shouldest set in order the things that are wanting,... ": **(Titus 1:5)**

1. START by having the CHURCH APPOINT a VISITATION COMMITTEE.

A COMMITTEE OF THREE is large enough to get results. One is appointed CHAIRMAN of the VISITATION COMMITTEE to keep the plan rolling and in order.

2. START by having the VISITATION COMMITTEE SELECT GROUP LEADERS to keep records at all services.

The VISITATION COMMITTEE also appoints HELPERS for each of the GROUP LEADERS.

3. START by having ALL PERSONS possible who are qualified.

To serve in this plan, EACH PERSON should be a MEMBER in good and regular standing in the local church in question. They should also appreciate this opportunity for service in this way (see SECTION #4)

4. START by having the VISITATION OFFICE lineup calls or SPECIAL VISITS for various GROUP LEADERS and HELPERS when needed (See SECTION #6 for various calls.)

5. START by realizing the SPECIFIC NUMBERS that will be needed in your particular local church.

In a church of 100 members, this would represent about 30 families (on the average). This means that the VISITATION COMMITTEE will appoint 10 GROUP LEADERS who will be responsible for THREE FAMILIES (about 10 people in all). These 10 GROUP LEADERS keep records on FORM #2.

GET THINGS DONE

This FORM #2 is one source of places to visit absentees from the various services of the church. (See SECTION #7, "Various Kinds of Calls.")

Each GROUP LEADER reports on FORM #3 twice each month as to what the results have been.

VISITATION CHAIRMAN sees to it that records are kept so as to get the best and most results. See to it that covers for record books and FORMS #1, #2, and #3 are on HAND AT ALL TIMES. (These are ordered from THE BIBLE FOR TODAY.)

IT'S THE FOLLOW-UP THAT COUNTS MOST!

PLAN YOURWORK—AND WORK YOUR PLAN!

CALL WEEKLY AND REGULARLY—by PERSON by PHONE, by LETTER (see SECTION #6)

THE BIG JOB IS TO KEEP ALL THE IRONS IN THE FIRE AND KEEP THEM ALL HOT!

SECTION XII

THINGS TO DO

WORK OUT DETAILS

*"Moreover it is required in stewards, that a man be found FAITHFUL." **(1 Corinthians 4:2)***

GROUP LEADERS are appointed by the VISITATION CHAIRMAN or the VISITATION COMMITTEE, and they are approved by the local church for the purpose of promoting this plan of VISITATION IN ACTION.

Appoint one GROUP LEADER for every THREE FAMILIES. This will represent an average of about 10 persons per GROUP LEADER. Each GROUP LEADER fills out FORM #2 (see SECTION #25) every Sunday. This form permits the GROUP LEADER to keep an up-to-date record of each individual member for whom he is responsible. It gives him the reason to make a personal visit or whatever is needed.

FORM #2—GIVES YOU YOUR CUE!

At the close of EACH SUNDAY SERVICE each GROUP LEADER turns in the VISITATION OFFICE the NAMES OF ABSENTEES for whom he is responsible (of his 3 families, or about 10 people), so that arrangements can be made for CONTACTS before a new week starts.

The GROUP LEADERS should contact EACH ONE on their lists who is absent and try to get that person active again. (see SECTION #15).

GROUP LEADERS and HELPERS should also act like a WELCOMING COMMITTEE anytime they see a VISITOR in church or Bible School. Give the visitor a hardy WELCOME. Jot down his name and address for your follow up.

GROUP LEADERS and HELPERS should be organized in various parts of the church so there is not a lot of running around as you greet visitors. Using "VISITATION IN ACTION "will increase attendance, so there will be MORE VISITORS TO WELCOME!

SUGGESTIONS TO THE CHAIRMAN

Occasionally, have a meeting of all workers, GROUP LEADERS and HELPERS. Use "VISITATION IN ACTION" as your textbook.

Here are a few suggestions: Teach your workers how to do various phases of VISITATION as listed in the book, such as passing of tracts, how to canvass streets, how to invite people to services, and how to tell the salvation story.

All of these different approaches are parts of the whole picture. Go to different parts of the book at different meetings. Show these leaders in VISITATION how to keep records and also show them how to fill out FORMS #1, #2, and #3 (SECTION XXIV).

IT'S TEAMWORK AND COOPERATION THAT GETS IT DONE!

SECTION XIII

THERE HAS TO BE A "BOSS"

"Not slothful in business; fervent in spirit; serving the Lord;" ***(Romans 12:11)***

In this case, the "BOSS" is the CHAIRMAN. A "CHAIRMAN" (or a "BOSS") is someone who knows what to do and DOES IT. He also gets others to FOLLOW THROUGH.

A CHAIRMAN must use ALL his InItIatIve. (Note the four "I's" in "initiative.") The following are the "FOUR I's" of initiative that each CHAIRMAN must keep in mind if he is to succeed in his job of VISITATION IN ACTION:

1. I HAVE A JOB TO DO --- ACTION (Read SECTION IV, IX, XI).

   The CHAIRMAN is continually RECRUITING for more WORKERS to meet the needs. As the work grows, more HELP is needed. PLAN on GROWTH and replacements. (Read SECTIONS XII, XV, and XVI.)

2. I HAVE TO KEEP THE PLAN MOVING and see to it that everyone is DOING THEIR JOB --- ACTION (See SECTIONS V, and VI.)

   "VISITATION IN ACTION" is a continuous plan. It's like a spring-fed well. It never runs dry. There is ALWAYS SOMEONE TO VISIT. It's an EVERLASTING PLAN.

3. I HAVE TO SEE THAT EVERYTHING IS IN ORDER.

ANALYZE, PLAN, WORK. Records should be kept of names, addresses, phone numbers, of adults and children. Get all information available.

Many CALL-BACKS can be made from good records and people can be won. RECORDS determine PROGRESS. RECORDS tell where CHANGES should be made. It's FINDING a way and MAKING a way as you move forward.

4. I HAVE TO KEEP ENTHUSIASTIC AND KEEP EVERTHING UNDER CONTROL AS I DEAL WITH PEOPLE.

Develop a "NEVER GIVE UP" attitude. Learn these three little words:

"YES YOU CAN"

G O O D L E A D E R S A R E G O O D F O L L O W E R S

SECTION XIV

MORE INSTRUCTIONS

*"Whoso loveth INSTRUCTION loveth knowledge: but he that hateth reproof is brutish." **(Proverbs 12:1)***

"NO SHORT CUTS IN VISITATION"

A GROUP LEADER should see to it that when anyone on his list is ABSENT, a SPECIAL CALL should be made. Deliver a Church Bulletin, a special message of being missed at whatever service was missed (according to your records). Make it REAL. Make it TRUE. Have a PURPOSE.

Each GROUP LEADER can request from the VISITATION COMMITTEE some HELPERS as the need for HELPERS arises for making calls, phoning people, or mailing letters

WATCH WHAT YOU SAY, AND
HOW YOU SAY IT!

RECORDS ARE KEPT THAT ONE MIGHT LEARN WHAT IS NEEDED AND THEN DO SOMETHING ABOUT IT.

KEEP RECORDS FOR BIRTHDAYS, ANNIVERSARIES, CHRISTIAN BIRTHDAYS, and ANY UNUSUAL THING. THESE ARE JUST ANOTHER OPPORTUNITY TO MAKE A CALL, OR MAIL A CARD, AND GAIN A FRIEND.

SECTION XV

GROUP LEADERS

"Pray ye therefore the Lord of the harvest, that he will send forth labourers into his harvest." ***(Matthew 9:38)***

Each GROUP LEADER is to be at EVERY SERVICE of the local church! The BLIND cannot lead the BLIND, or they will both fall into the ditch.

RECORDS are to be checked for every service on every member for whom the GROUP LEADER is responsible. See FORM #2. From these records you will know on whom to call and what to do. (See SECTION #9, ITEM #4.)

Read Hebrews 10:25 again. Note these words:
"NOT FORSAKING"
"AS THE MANNER OF SOME"
"BUT EXHORTING ONE ANOTHER."

This word, "exhorting," means to "ENCOURAGE," "CHALLENGE," or "CHECK UP ON." And "so much the more" as we are in these last days.

So every GROUP LEADER and every HELPER have to be very TACTFUL, very GRACIOUS, and extra KIND as they approach folks who have neglected "so great salvation" (Hebrews 2:3) and to others who know not the way of salvation.

The Holy Spirit will direct you. Be sure to read Colossians 4:6. See what a HELPER does (See Section #16).

SECTION XVI

WHAT IS A HELPER?

"That ye submit yourselves unto such, and to every one that helpeth with us, and laboureth." **(1 Corinthians 16:16)**

Y
E
S

Y
O
U

C
A
N

1. A HELPER is one who works with the GROUP LEADER in contacting absentees.

2. A HELPER WELCOMES the VISITORS at all services.

3. A HELPER CALLS on any who need to be called on as directed by the VISITATION COMMITTEE.

4. A HELPER works and COOPERATES with his GROUP LEADER in any phase of the VISITATION plan.

5. A HELPER REPORTS to his GROUP LEADER what has been accomplished.

6. A HELPER MAILS a Church Bulletin to any of the members for whom he is responsible when that member is out of town, or else address the envelope in care of that member, and hands it to the VISITATION CHAIRMAN or any member of the VISITATION COMMITTEE to mail.

LEARN HOW TO CALL BY CALLLING.

IT WORKS. BUT IT TAKES YOU TO WORK IT.

WEIGH EACH WORD YOU USE WHEN DEALING WITH PEOPLE.

SECTION XVII

"BUS" MINISTRY

T
H
E
R
E

M
U
S
T

B
E

A

C
H
I
E
F

"Go out quickly into the streets and lanes of the city, ... " ***(Luke 14:21)***

"BUS" MINISTRY is a CREATIVE plan of visiting people in given neighborhoods and can be worked with GROUP LEADERS and their HELPERS.

1. BUS TERRITORY should be assigned so that there is no over-lapping.

The territories must be canvassed and records must be kept of every call made. Get names, addresses, phone numbers, and other information from every person contacted. Jot down on a card all the information you can get. Keep the card file for every home. From your files you can make call-backs and build your BUS ROUTES.

2. BUS TERRITORY must be VISITED on the SATURDAY before the Sunday BUS PICK-UP. Know what to do and where to go.

Successful BUS ROUTES are built by contacting the prospects on the SATURDAY before the SUNDAY BUS RUNS are made. Again, good records must be kept so you can have a plan to work from. You then can analyze the records to see how your plan is working, making changes, when necessary. Successful BUS MINISTRY is a CONTINUAL CALLING JOB! See other pages on how to canvass.

SUCCESS IS JUST AROUND THE CORNER.
YOUR JOB IS TO GET TO THE CORNER!
THIS TAKES WORK and PLANS.

SECTION XVIII

BUILDING A LARGER BIBLE SCHOOL

"... for the people had a mind to work." ***(Nehemiah 4:6)***

1. FIND THEM!

    a. LOOK FOR THEM. Where? Everywhere. In homes of all descriptions.

    b. LEARN that EVERYBODY'S your PROSPECT.

2. FIND WAYS or MAKE WAYS!
    a. Learn how to CREATE calls!

    b. Secure information on ALL visitors in your class each Sunday.

    c. Invite your neighbors and associates every week to Bible Class and church services.

    d. Speak to visitors in the worship services when you see them.

3. FETCH THEM!
    How can you "fetch them"? By bus or in your own car.

    a. VISIT prospective members often.

    b. OFFER to BRING THEM to Bible School and make definite plans to pick them up.

    c. KEEP AFTER the absentees. Don't give up. Keep trying to get them out on a REGULAR basis—with all the tact that you can muster. This is no easy job.

4. FEED THEM!

What? Feed them God's Word. This is a job for the GROUP LEADER to do.

a. BE FRIENDLY. Let them know the joy of Christian fellowship.

b. GET THEM ACTIVE in class activities.

c. DISCUSS God's Word with them.

d. BE A GOOD WITNESS. Tell them what the Lord Jesus Christ has done for you.

HAVE GOALS—PLAN ON SPECIAL DAYS.
GET EXCITED!

Every month of the year promote a "BIG SUNDAY." Give the GROUP LEADERS a job to do. They start to call, visit, phone, and do other necessary things 30 days before the "BIG DAY." When you get through with one "BIG SUNDAY," you start working on the next one. This goes on 12 months of the year. No slack seasons. No lay-offs. Just KEEP ON KEEPING ON. No excuses. YES YOU CAN!

PLAN ON MORE THAN YOU CAN DO, AND DO IT!

SECTION XIX

MANY REASONS FOR ATTENDING BIBLE SCHOOL

"Rooted and built up in him, and STABLISHED in the faith,..." ***(Colossians 2:7)***

1. GODLINESS. It teaches the Bible, which is the basis of our faith in God and leads to Christ as personal Savior and Lord.

2. EDUCATION. It trains your mind and heart along the line of things eternal.

3. SOCIETY. It enables you to enjoy the friendship of genuine Christians.

4. PERSONALITY. It helps to develop the Christian's character necessary to face life's problems victoriously.

5. CHARACTER. It is the chief aim of the Bible School to teach us to be examples of the believer in word and deed.

6. INTEREST. It presents interesting programs for your delight and culture.

7. FAMILY. It has a class for every age, and the whole family can go together and profit by its teachings.

8. SERVICE. It affords ample opportunity to serve God and the local church in activities that are not open elsewhere.

9. IMMORTALITY. It turns our eyes Heavenward and makes us realize that we must prepare for a life beyond the mortal grave.

10. PRACTICALITY. The hour or so spent in Bible School each Sunday could not be expended more profitably. (Proverbs 22:6)

All we can do is to show the way. Some SCRIPTURES we can use are as follows:

John 6:44	
HOW TO BE SAVED	ROAD TO SALVATION
1. **Galatians 1:4** Who gave himself for our sins, that he might deliver us from this present evil world, according to the will of God and our Father: **(Galatians 1:4)**	1. FACT OF SIN For all have sinned, and come short of the glory of God; **(Romans 3:23)**
2. **John 8:24** I said therefore unto you, that ye shall die in your sins: for if ye believe not that I am *he*, ye shall die in your sins. **(John 8:24)**	2. PENALTY OF SIN For the wages of sin *is* death; but the gift of God *is* eternal life through Jesus Christ our Lord. **(Romans 6:23)**
3. Romans 10:13 For whosoever shall call upon the name of the Lord shall be saved. **(Romans 10:13)**	3. PENALTY MUST BE PAID And as it is appointed unto men once to die, but after this the judgment: **(Hebrews 9:27)**
4. Acts 4:12 Neither is there salvation in any other: for there is none other name under heaven given among men, whereby we must be saved. **(Acts 4:12)**	4. PENALTY PAID BY CHRIST But God commendeth his love toward us, in that, while we were yet sinners, Christ died for us. **(Romans 5:8)**
5. John 14:6 Jesus saith unto him, I am the way, the truth, and the life: no man cometh unto the Father, but by me. **(John 14:6)**	5. SALVATION A FREE GIFT For by grace are ye saved through faith; and that not of yourselves: *it is* the gift of God:

	Not of works, lest any man should boast. **(Ephesians 2:8-9)**
6. Romans 3:23 For all have sinned, and come short of the glory of God; **(Romans 3:23)**	6. GIFT MUST BE RECEIVED But as many as received him, to them gave he power to become the sons of God, *even* to them that believe on his name: **(John 1:12)**
7. John 3:16-18 For God so loved the world, that he gave his only begotten Son, that whosoever believeth in him should not perish, but have everlasting life. For God sent not his Son into the world to condemn the world; but that the world through him might be saved. He that believeth on him is not condemned: but he that believeth not is condemned already, because he hath not believed in the name of the only begotten Son of God. **(John 3:16-18)**	
8. Romans 10:9 That if thou shalt confess with thy mouth the Lord Jesus, and shalt believe in thine heart that God hath raised him from the dead, thou shalt be saved. **(Romans 10:9)**	

"FAITH COMETH BY HEARING, AND HEARING BY THE WORD OF GOD."

Use your BIBLE when leading a person to the saving knowledge of Jesus Christ. (See SECTION #5)

We suggest you use the KING JAMES VERSION preferably, rather than the so-called “modern speech” versions and “translations” or “paraphrases.”

NOTHING TAKES THE PLACE OF WORK

SECTION XX

A GOOD BEGINNING

"The night is far spent, the day is at hand:...". ***(Romans 13:12)***

DEACONS, TRUSTEES, TEACHERS, OFFICERS COMMITTEE HEADS all give your church a GOOD START on your VISITATION IN ACTION as outlined in SECTION #11.

These preceding groups are already "church-approved." Select a CHAIRMAN and GET THE PROGRAM INTO ACTION TODAY! Don't wait for tomorrow to do something you can do TODAY! Time is running out. It's what is done TODAY that counts.

Regardless of what kind of a VISITATION plan your church has, you'll find many things in "VISITATION IN ACTION" you'll profit from.

The time is NOW to put on your VISION GLASSES. Take a good look at all the people all around you and look at those in the church too. Some never take time or have time for the things of the Lord.

Most outsiders never received a Christian tract or a call from a Bible-believing church. It's your OPPORTUNITY!

"Awake to righteousness, and sin not; for some have not the knowledge of God: I speak this to your shame."
(1 Corinthians 15:34)

KEEP YOUR MIND OPEN FOR CHANGES THAT ARE WORKABLE IN THE LORD'S WORK.

"IF" your VISITATION PROGRAM is not showing INCREASES in personnel and it's the same "FAITHFUL FEW," why not try some different methods.

You have EVERYTHING TO GAIN. Watch the NEW INTEREST and GROWTH!

Don't let you VISITATION PROGRAM get in a RUT!

A RUT is difficult to get out of. When in a RUT, one does not go FAR or FAST.

"IF" you want to develop workers and "IF" you want to INCREASE your ATTENDANCE, RE-READ "VISITATION IN ACTION" and use some of these ideas that you are not now using.

It won't be long before you'll see the RESULTS.

Start at once to get ready to BE READY for INCREASES!

SECTION XXI

CONTACTING PEOPLE

He that believeth on him is not condemned: but he that believeth not is condemned already, because he hath not believed in the name of the only begotten Son of God. ***(John 3:18)***

You will be dealing with two classes of people: (1) The LOST (unbelievers); and (2) The SAVED (believers).

REASON—"All have sinned" (Romans 3:23)

REMEDY—"The GIFT of God" (Romans 6:23)

IN CANVASSING, THERE IS AN ENDLESS OPPORTUNITY TO WITNESS.

There are at least three types of "CONTACTS" you can make with people; (1) PASSING TRACTS TO THEM; (2) INVITING THEM TO THE SERVICES; (3) TELLING THEM THE PLAN OF SALVATION.

1. PASSING TRACTS. The largest percentage of people, when canvassing, will turn out to be unbelievers. An easy beginning, in learning to meet people, is to start with tracts, passing these out from door to door, store to store, office to office—EVERYWHERE. Always have a supply with you. See the VISITATION CHAIRMAN for the right kinds of tracts to use.

   When going door to door, you rap on the door. When the door is opened, you hand the person a tract saying "I have a Christian tract for your home. I do hope you'll read it. Thank you." Then you go away to the next place. This is quick and to the point. KEEP RECORDS of these calls.

2. INVITING TO SERVICES. After you have done this a few dozen times, you'll start to learn something about people. Also, you'll learn what to do when you call back the second time. This time, you go a little further in your approach. Give the person another tract and at the same time, INVITE THEMTO THE SERVICES of the Church. RECORD this information also.

3. THE PLAN OF SALVATION. From these calls and the information about the family you have recorded, you now have a firm basis on a third visit to speak to them about God's plan of Salvation, showing them how to become a believer in the Lord Jesus Christ.

> KNOW WHAT TO SAY AND LEARN HOW TO SAY WHAT YOU KNOW.

(SECTION XIX, "HOW TO BE SAVED" and "THE ROAD TO SALVATION")

SECTION XXII

CREATING A DESIRE

"...The harvest truly is plenteous,..." **(Matthew 9:37)**

Y E S

Y O U

C A N

Every home is a PROSPECT for Bible School and church. Most homes are also prospects for salvation through faith in the Lord Jesus Christ.

That's where you, as a GROUP LEADER or HELPER, do your job. Just follow the steps outlined:

STEP #1. YOU HAVE LEFT A TRACT (First call).

STEP #2. YOU HAVE CALLED BACK. This could be a week or two later. You now leave another tract, but this time, you find out a little more about the home you're visiting. By this time, you have the names of the people within. You ask a few questions, such as, "Do you attend any church or Bible School?" Regardless of their answer, you give them a BIG enthusiastic welcome to come to your church. Even offer to "FETCH" them. You are out to WIN THEM, so WATCH YOUR STEP! (Second call).

STEP #3. YOU TELL THEM ABOUT SALVATION. Maybe nothing has worked up to now. But it's time to make another call. This time, as the Spirit leads you, you come with your Bible to show them (this family), the PLAN OF SALVATION. (See Section #19). (Third call.)

Don't become discouraged!

A WINNER NEVER QUITS,
AND A QUITTER NEVER WINS!

REMEMBER

VISITATION has no slack seasons.

VISITATION has no lay-offs.

VISITATION has no shut-downs.

VISITATION operates as long as there are people. As long as there are people, there will be a NEED to VISIT! (Read page 13)

Make the MOST of these EXTRA PLUS HELPS in dealing with people as you use your copy of "VISITATION IN ACTION."

SECTION XXIII

WHAT TO DO WITH ABSENTEES

"As we have therefore opportunity, let us do good unto all men, especially unto them who are of the household of faith." **(Galatians 6:10)**

There are two types of "saved" people. Both of them have made a profession of faith in Christ as their Savior, but one type puts FIRST THINGS FIRST. The other type only comes occasionally to Bible School or church services.

Your work as a GROUP LEADER or HELPER is to do all you can to ENCOURAGE these folks to be REGULAR attendees. Give them literature, a church bulletin, a warm welcome, a word of prayer, and a verse of Scripture.

YOUR GOAL—TO WIN EVERY ABSENTEE ON YOUR ROLL! This is not easy, Do every little thing you can do to bring this to pass.

Keep after them EVERY WEEK until you see them in services. Each time you call on them bring a bulletin and literature, and give them a Bible verse for them to think about.

They might get tired of seeing you come, BUT don't you get tired of going to them. (Galatians 6:9).

REMEMBER—IT'S THE CONSTANT DRIPPING OF A DROP OF WATER THAT WEARS THE MIGHTY ROCK!

GOD SAYS (in Hebrews 4:12) *"FOR THE WORD OF GOD IS QUICK, AND POWERFUL, AND SHARPER than any twoedged sword, piercing even to the dividing asunder of soul and spirit, and of the joints and marrow, and is a discerner of the thoughts and intents of the heart."*

LEARN HOW TO USE IT!

SECTION XXIV

VISITATION ENLISTMENT CARD

"That ye might walk worthy of the Lord unto all pleasing, being fruitful in every good work, and increasing in the knowledge of God;" **(Colossians 1:10)**

FORM #1

In response to the call for SERVICE in personal VISITATION, I hereby accept my RESPONSIBILITY and "as much as in me is" (*"So, as much as in me is, I am ready to preach the gospel to you ..."*. **(Romans 1:15)** I SURRENDER all my personal abilities and my powers for Him for VISITATION in connection with the

____

(Name of the Church)

NAME: ______________________________________

ADDRESS: ____________________________________

PHONE:____________________DATE:______________

<u>SCHEDULE</u> <u>OF</u> <u>AVAILABILITY</u>

Day of Week Mornings Afternoon Evenings

(Please Give Times)

Sunday:______________________________________

Monday:______________________________________

Tuesday:_____________________________________

Wednesday:___________________________________

Thursday:____________________________________

Friday:______________________________________

Saturday:____________________________________

SECTION XXV

WEEKLY TALLY FOR YOUR TEN PEOPLE

FORM #2

GROUP LEADER'S NAME:______________________________

DATE:____________________BOOK#:____________________

RECORD OF YOUR ROLL OF TEN PEOPLE:

NAME	ADDRESS	BIBLE SCHOOL	A.M. SERVICE	P.M. SERVICE	WED. PRAYER	LORD'S TABLE	YOUNG PEOPLE	TOTALS:	PERSONAL VISIT	PHONE CALL	BULLETIN MAILED	NEW CONTACTS	TOTALS:
1.													
2.													
3.													
4.													
5.													
6.													
7.													
8.													
9.													
10													
	TOTALS:												

SECTION XXVI

GROUP LEADER'S REPORT

FORM #3

GROUP LEADERS NAME: ADDRESS BOOK # / DATE:	WEEK #1	DATE:	WEEK #2	DATE:	WEEK #3	DATE:	WEEK #4	DATE:	WEEK #5	DATE:	GRAND TOTALS:
A. TOTAL VISITS PERSONALLY:											
B. TOTAL BULLETINS MAILED:											
C. TOTAL BULLETINS PERSONALLY DELIVERED											
D. TOTAL NEW CONTACTS MADE:											
E. TOTAL PHONE CALLS MADE											
TOTALS:											

(Fill in totals at close of each month and give to VISITATION CHAIRMAN.)

"OUR DESIRE, OUR AIM—EVERY MEMBER IN EVRY SERVICE!"

"FOR WE ARE LABORERS TOGETHER WITH GOD."

SECTION XXVII

YOUR SUGGESTIONS

If, as you work with this "VISITATION IN ACTION" program, you can see certain suggestions for making it better, both in the local church, or in other churches that might be using this plan, you are invited to jot down YOUR SUGGESTIONS below, and give them to the VISITATION CHAIRMAN of your church, or send them to the AUTHOR in care of the PUBLISHER of this booklet: THE BIBLE FOR TODAY, 900 Park Avenue, Collingswood, NJ, 08108:

1.
2.
3.
4.
5.
6.
7.
8.
9.
10.

SECTION XXVIII

SCRIPTURES TO READ--INDEX

A. OLD TESTAMENT VERSES

B. NEW TESTAMENT VERSES

10. 8:24	p. 54
11. 14:6	p. 54
12. Acts 1:8	p. 29
13. 2:42-47	p. 11
14. 2:47	p. 19
15. 4:12	p. 25
16. Romans 3:23	p. 54
17. 5:8	p. 54
18. 3:23	pp. 54, 55, 59, 72.
19. 5:8	pp. 54, 72,
20. 6:23	pp. 54, 59
21. 8:24	pp. 54
22. 8:28	pp. 15
23. 10:13	pp. 12, 54
24. 10:17	pp. 17
25. 12:1	pp. 15
26. 12:11	p. 41
27. 13:12	p. 57
28. 1 Corinthians 3:9	p. 21
29. 4:2	p. 39
30. 12:31	p. 25
31. 14:40	p. 33
32. 15:34	p. 57
33. 15:58	p. 57
34. 16:16	p. 47
35. 2 Corinthians 5:11	p. 17
36. 9:7	p. 14
37. 13:5	p. 15
38. Galatians 1:4	p. 54
39. 6:9	p. 63
40. 6:10	p. 63
41. Ephesians 2:8-9	p. 55
42. Philippians 4:13	p. 15
43. Colossians 1:10	p. 65

44. 2:7	p. 53
45. 4:6	pp. 27, 45
46. 2 Timothy 2:15	p. 15
47. Titus 1:5	p. 37
48. Hebrews 2:3	p. 45
49. 4:12	p. 64
50. 6:12	p. 35
51. 9:27	p. 54
52. 10:25	p. 45
53. James 1:22	p. 17

INDEX OF WORDS

ORDER BLANK (P. 1)

Name:____

Address:______________________________________

City and State:________________________Zip________

Credit Card #:_________________Expires_______CC#____

Latest Books

[ ] Send *The Sixth 200 Questions Answered* By Dr. D. A. Waite (188 pp. perfect bound $15.00 + $7.00 S & H)

[ ] Send *The Fifth 200 Questions Answered* By Dr. D. A. Waite (150 pp. perfect bound $15.00 + $7.00 S & H)

[ ] Send *The Fourth 200 Questions Answered* By Dr. D. A. Waite (168 pp. perfect bound $15.00 + $7.00 S & H)

[ ] Send *The Third 200 Questions Answered* By Dr. D. A. Waite (180 pp. perfect bound $15.00 + $7.00 S & H)

[ ] Send *The Second 200 Questions Answered* By Dr. D. A. Waite (178 pp. perfect bound $15.00 + $7.00 S & H)

[ ] Send *The First 200 Questions Answered* By Dr. D. A. Waite (184 pp. perfect bound $12.00 + $7.00 S & H)

[ ] Send *A Critical Answer to James Price's King James Onlyism* By Pastor D. A. Waite, 184 pp, perfect bound ($11 + $7 S&H)

[ ] Send *The KJB's Superior Hebrew & Greek Words* By Pastor D. A. Waite, 104 pp., perfect bound ($10.00+$7 S&H)

[ ] Send *Soulwinning's Versions-Perversions* By Pastor D. A. Waite, booklet, 28 pp. ($6+$5 S&H)

[ ] Send *2 Timothy—Preaching Verse By Verse*, By Pastor D. A. Waite, 250 pp. perfect bound ($11+$7 S&H)

[ ] Send *A Critical Answer to God's Word Preserved* By Pastor D. A. Waite, 192 pp., perfect bound ($11.00+$7 S&H)

[ ] Send *Daily Bible Blessings* By Yvonne Waite ($20+$8 S&H)

[ ] Send *Revelation—Preaching Verse By Verse* By Dr. D. A. Waite ($50+$10 S&H—1030 pages.

Send or Call Orders to:
THE BIBLE FOR TODAY
900 Park Ave., Collingswood, NJ 08108
Phone: 856-854-4452; FAX:--2464; Orders: 1-800 JOHN 10:9
Email Orders: BFT@BibleForToday.org; Credit Cards OK

ORDER BLANK (P. 2)

Name:____

Address:____

City and State:_________________________Zip______

Credit Card #:____________________Expires______CC#____

[ ] Send *The Occult Connections of Gail Riplinger* By Dr. Phil Stringer ($12 + $7 S & H)

[ ] Send *A WARNING!! On Gail Riplinger's KJB & Multiple Inspiration Heresy,* By Pastor D. A. Waite (133 pp. perfect bound $12 + $7 S & H)

[ ] Send *Who Is Gail Riplinger?* By Aleithia O'Brien, 146 pp., (12.00+$7.00S&H)

[ ] Send *The Messianic Claims of Gail A. Riplinger,* By Dr. Phil Stringer, 108 pp. perfect bound ($12+$7 S&H)

[ ] Send *Husband Loving Lessons* By Dr. Yvonne S. Waite; A very valuable marriage manual (294 pp. perfect bound, $25+$7 S&H)

[ ] Send *8,000 Differences Between The Textus Receptus & Critical Text* By Dr. J. A. Moorman (544 pp. hardback ($20.00 + $7.00S&H)

[ ] Send *Early Manuscripts, Church Fathers, & The Authorized Version* By Dr. Jack Moorman, ($20+#7 S&H, Hardback)
By Pastor D. A. Waite, 184 pp, perfect bound ($11 + $7 S&H)

[ ] Send *The The LIE That Changed the Modern World* By Dr. H. D Williams ($16+$7 S&H)

[ ] Send *With Tears In My Heart* By Gertrude G. Sanborn, Hardback, 414 pp. ($25+$7 S&H) 400 Christian Poems.

Preaching Verse by Verse Books

[ ] Send *2 Timothy—Preaching Verse By Verse,* By Pastor D. A. Waite, 250 pp. perfect bound ($11+$7 S&H) fully indexed.

[ ] Send *1 Timothy—Preaching Verse By Verse,* By Pastor D. A. Waite, 288 pp., Hardback ($14.00+$7 S&H) fully indexed.

[ ] Send *Romans—Preaching Verse By Verse By Pastor D. A.* Waite 736 pp. Hardback ($25+$7 S&H) fully indexed.

[ ] Send *Revelation—Preaching Verse By Verse* By Dr. D. A. Waite ($50+$10 S&H—1030pages.

Send or Call Orders to:
THE BIBLE FOR TODAY
900 Park Ave., Collingswood, NJ 08108
Phone: 856-854-4452; FAX:--2464; Orders: 1-800 JOHN 10:9
Email Orders: BFT@BibleForToday.org; Credit Cards OK

ORDER BLANK (P. 3)

Name:____

Address:____

City and State:_____________________________Zip______

Credit Card #:____________________Expires______CC#____

Preaching Verse by Verse Books

[ ] Send *Colossians & Philemon—Preaching Verse by Verse* By Pastor D. A. Waite ($12+$7 S&H) hardback, 240 pp.

[ ] Send *First Peter—Preaching Verse byVerse,* By Pastor D. A. Waite (176 pp. hardback, $10 + $7 S&H)

[ ] Send *Philippians—Preaching Verse by Verse* By Pastor D. A. Waite ($10+$7 S&H 176 pp., hardback)

[ ] Send *Ephesians—Preaching Verse by Verse* By Pastor D. A. Waite 224 pp. perfect bound ($12+$7 S&H)

[ ] Send *Galatians—Preaching Verse by Verse* By Pastor D. A. Waite; (216 pp. hardback, $13+$7 S&H)

Books on Bible Texts & Translations

[ ] Send *Defending the King James Bible* by DAW ($12+$7 S&H) A Hardback book, indexed with study questions

[ ] Send *BJU's Errors on Bible Preservation* By Dr. D. A. Waite, pp. 110, perfect bound ($8+$7 S&H) fully indexed.

[ ] Send *Fundamental Deception on Bible Preservation* By Dr. DAW ($8+$7 S&H) fully indexed.

[ ] Send *Fundamentalists MIS-INFORMATION on Bible Versions* By DAW ($7+$7 S&H perfect bound, 136 pp.)

[ ] Send *Fundamentalists Distortions on Bible Versions* By Pastor D. A. Waite, 136 pp. perfect bound ($7+$5 S&H) fully indexed.

[ ] Send *Fuzzy Facts From Fundamentalists* By Pastor D. A. Waite, ($8.00+$7 S&H) fully indexed

More Books on Bible Texts & Translations

[ ] Send *Foes of the King James Bible Refuted By Pastor D. A.* Waite (164 pp. $8+$7 S&H) fully indexed.

[ ] Send *Central Seminary Refuted on Bible Versions* By Dr. D. A. Waite ($10+$7 S&H) 184 pages.

Send or Call Orders to:
THE BIBLE FOR TODAY
900 Park Ave., Collingswood, NJ 08108
Phone: 856-854-4452; FAX:--2464; Orders: 1-800 JOHN 10:9
Email Orders: BFT@BibleForToday.org; Credit Cards OK

ORDER BLANK (P. 4)

Name:____

Address:____

City and State:_________________________________**Zip**______

Credit Card #:____________________**Expires**______**CC#**____

Preaching Verse by Verse Books

[ ] Send *The Case for the King James Bible* By Pastor D. A. Waite ($8+$5 S&H) perfect bound, 112 pp.

[ ] Send T*heological Heresies of Westcott and Hort,* By Pastor D. A. Waite ($8 + $5 S&H)

[ ] Send *Westcott's Denial of Resurrection,* By Pastor D. A. Waite ($8 + $5 S&H)

[ ] Send *Four Reasons for Defending the KJB* By Pastor D. A. Waite ($4+$3 S&H)

More Books on Bible Texts & Translations

[ ] Send *Holes in the Holman Christian Standard Bible* by Dr. D. A. Waite ($6+$4 S&H) A printed booklet, 40 pages

[ ] Send C*ontemporary English Version Exposed* By Dr. D. A. Waite, ($6+$4 S&H)

[ ] Send *NIV Inclusive Language Exposed* By Dr. D. A. Waite ($7+$5 S&H) fully indexed.

[ ] Send *24 Hours of KJB Seminar (4 DVD's)* By DAW ($50+$10 S&H)

Books By Dr. Jack Moorman

[ ] Send *Manuscript Digest of the N.T.* By Dr. Jack Moorman, (721 pp. copy machine bound ($50+$10 S&H) fully indexed.

[ ] Send *Early Manuscripts, Church Fathers, & The Authorized Version* By Dr. Jack Moorman, ($20+#7 S&H, Hardback)

[ ] Send *When the KJB Departs from the So-called "Majority Text"* By Dr. Jack Moorman ($17.00+$7.00 S&H)

More Books By Dr. Jack Moorman

[ ] Send *Missing in Modern Bibles—Nestle/Aland/NIV Errors* By Dr. Jack Moorman ($8+$7 S&H)

[ ] Send *the Doctrinal Heart of the Bible—Removed from Modern Versions* By Dr. Jack Moorman, VCR, $15+$7 S&H ($10+$7 S&H 184 pages.

Send or Call Orders to:
THE BIBLE FOR TODAY
900 Park Ave., Collingswood, NJ 08108
Phone: 856-854-4452; FAX:--2464; Orders: 1-800 JOHN 10:9
Email Orders: BFT@BibleForToday.org; Credit Cards OK

www.ingramcontent.com/pod-product-compliance
Lightning Source LLC
Chambersburg PA
CBHW071456070426
42452CB00040B/1543

* 9 7 8 1 5 6 8 4 8 0 8 9 3 *